HELEN
KELLER

HELEN KELLER

Margaret Davidson

Illustrated by Wendy Watson

SCHOLASTIC INC.
New York Toronto London Auckland Sydney

For Bill Haber
who also sees with his heart

ISBN 0-590-42404-1

Text copyright © 1969 by Margaret Davidson. Illustrations copyright © 1969 by Wendy Watson. All rights reserved. Published by Scholastic Inc.

12   3 4/9

Contents

A Strange Fever

THE BEGINNING was happy for Helen. She laughed and loved and grew like any other baby. First she crawled, then she walked, and she was learning to talk. Each day was full of adventures.

Then everything stopped. One day Helen laughed and played as usual. The next day she lay tossing and turning in bed. She was very, very sick. The doctor was called. But he could do little to help. A strange fever was burning her up.

Probably Helen had scarlet fever. Today there are medicines that would have made her well. But Helen was born almost one hundred years ago — before these medicines were discovered.

So day after day Helen grew weaker. The doctor could not give her mother and father much hope. Helen Keller was only eighteen months old. The doctor was sure that she could not live much longer.

Then suddenly the fever fell. Helen seemed to be getting better. Mr. and Mrs. Keller sighed with relief. "Everything will be all right now," the doctor said.

But it wasn't.

Helen slept for many hours. When she woke again it was morning. The sun was shining in through the window. Sunlight splashed across her bed.

Mrs. Keller bent over her little girl. She smiled and waved her hand in front of Helen's face. Helen's eyes were wide open, but she didn't blink.

That was strange. Mrs. Keller waved her hand again — closer to Helen's eyes. Helen stared straight ahead.

Now Mrs. Keller grabbed a lamp. She shone its bright light right into Helen's eyes. Helen kept on staring.

Helen's mother began to scream. "Helen's blind! She can't see. My baby's blind!"

One morning soon after, Mrs. Keller dressed Helen and sat her down in the middle of the bedroom floor. Just then a loud bell in the back yard began to ring.

This was the Keller family's signal for meals. And Helen loved to eat. Whenever she heard the bell she trotted to the table as fast as she could. But now she did nothing. Nothing at all.

Mrs. Keller was making Helen's bed. "Helen?" she said. "*Helen?*" But Helen didn't move.

Mrs. Keller picked up a can of stones — one of Helen's toys. She rattled it in Helen's ear. Helen didn't even turn her head.

Then her mother knew. This time she didn't scream. She just bent and gathered Helen in her arms. "My baby's *deaf* too," she whispered.

The Dark Silence

THE DOCTOR looked at Helen. He shook his head. "There is nothing I can do," he said.

But Helen's father and mother refused to give up hope so easily. Tuscumbia, Alabama, was a very small town. And this was the only doctor there. So they took Helen to other doctors in other — bigger — towns. But the answer was always the same. "No hope."

Finally the Kellers understood that Helen would live all her life alone in dark silence.

She could not see the brightest light. She could not hear the loudest noise. Soon she forgot the words she had been learning. Then she became *dumb* — she could not speak at all.

Helen's body continued to grow. But how could her mind grow in the dark silence? There was so much she could no longer understand. She cried. But she didn't know she was sad. She screamed and kicked. But she didn't know she was angry. She smiled very seldom. She never laughed at all.

She wanted people to understand her, but she could not talk to them. She did not know any words. Helen didn't even know her own name. So now Helen began to make signs.

A nod meant *yes*. A shake of the head meant *no*. A pull meant *come*. A push meant *go away*. When Helen wanted something big she spread her hands wide — as if she were holding a big ball. When she wanted something small she took a tiny pinch of skin between two fingers.

When Helen wanted her mother she patted her own cheek and made a soft mewing sound.

Helen's father wore glasses. Helen liked to feel them — to take them off and put them on her father's nose. When she wanted her father she pretended to put on a pair of glasses too.

Soon Helen had sixty signs to tell people what she wanted.

Helen tried to find out about the world by touching everything she could. The Kellers lived on a small farm. Helen

loved to pat the horses and cows. Her
mother taught her how to feed the
chickens. Some grew so tame they ate
right out of her hand. Then Helen would
run her hands over their plump warm
bodies. She liked to touch anything that
moved. But there was so much she could
not really understand.

Helen put her fingers on her father's face and hands. She felt him holding a book. So Helen too held up a book in front of her face. But she didn't know what books were for.

She felt her mother pulling up weeds in the garden. So Helen tried to pull them up too. But how could she know the difference between a weed and a flower?

Worst of all were lips. Again and again Helen felt other peoples' lips moving. So she moved her lips too. But she didn't know what the moving lips meant.

What was everyone doing? What was going on? Helen became more and more angry. Sometimes the feeling of anger was more than she could stand. Then she kicked and screamed and tried to smash everything she touched. But this didn't help either. Helen grew even more angry. Soon not a day passed without a terrible temper tantrum.

There was so much she could not know! One day Helen spilled some water on her apron. She took it off and laid it down in front of the fireplace — but it did not dry fast enough to please her. She moved it closer and closer. Finally she laid the apron right on top of the flames.

The flames shot up through the apron — then to Helen's dress! Fire! She was on fire!

Helen screamed. Luckily someone was in the next room. The fire was put out before it did any harm.

"But she could have been killed," Mrs. Keller said.

"Or she could have burned the whole house down," Helen's father answered, "and us with it."

How much longer could this go on?

When Helen was five years old, her sister Mildred was born. All Helen knew about this baby was that it took up too much of her mother's time. Time that up until now had belonged to her!

Too often when Helen wanted to run into her mother's arms she found that the baby was already there. One day Helen reached out for her doll's cradle — and found the baby inside. This was too much! Helen growled like an animal. Then she reached out and knocked the cradle over. The baby fell screaming to the floor.

Luckily Mildred wasn't hurt. But what about next time? Helen was growing bigger and wilder every day.

"Next time she might really hurt the baby — or worse," Helen's father said. "No, I'm afraid there is only one thing we can do. We will have to send Helen away."

"Send her away?" Mrs. Keller cried. "Where would we send her?"

But she knew the answer herself. There was only one place that would take a wild creature like Helen — the State Insane Asylum!

"Let's wait just a little bit longer," Mrs. Keller begged.

Mr. Keller nodded. But they both knew that this was no real answer. They both knew that sooner or later Helen would have to be sent away.

Then one day Mrs. Keller read about a special school in Boston, Massachusetts, called Perkins Institute. Perkins was a school for the blind. But once, long ago, the teachers there had taught a little girl who was both blind *and* deaf. Somehow they had worked out a way to make her understand the outside world.

"Write to them," Mrs. Keller begged her husband. "Maybe they can help Helen too."

Helen's father shook his head. He had almost run out of hope. But that night he sat down and wrote a letter to Perkins Institute.

Now there was nothing else to do but wait.

The Stranger Comes

WHAT was going on? Helen had known all day that *something* was. The house had been cleaned from top to bottom — even the guest room had been opened and aired. Wonderful smells kept coming from the kitchen. And everyone was busy — much too busy to bother with her.

Late in the afternoon Helen felt her mother put on her hat and her gloves. Helen had learned long ago that this meant her mother was going somewhere. So she held onto her mother's skirt. She wanted to go too. But Mrs. Keller pulled away gently, and drove off in the carriage alone.

Whatever was going on, Helen didn't like it! She was six years old. But she had no words to tell how she felt. Every once in a while she shook her head sadly. And she waited.

For a long time nothing happened. Then suddenly Helen stood very still. She seemed to be listening as hard as she could. In a way she was. Not with her ears, but with her whole body.

Helen couldn't hear the loudest noise in the world. But sometimes she could feel things slam or shake around her. She could feel their *vibrations* coming through the air and the ground.

Now she felt the thud of horses' hoofs,

the vibration of carriage wheels coming back up the drive. The carriage stopped in front of the porch. Now Helen felt footsteps coming toward her across the porch floor. It must be her mother. Her mother was home at last! Helen held out her arms and felt herself being scooped up.

But this wasn't her mother! These were a stranger's arms!

The stranger was Miss Annie Sullivan. She had come all the way from Perkins Institute to try to help Helen. But of course Helen didn't know this. All she knew was that a stranger was holding her close. And Helen didn't like to be held by strangers.

So she kicked, she twisted, she tried to break free. But the stranger's arms only tightened around her! Helen began to growl.

"Let her go, Miss Annie!" Helen's
father cried. "Or she will hurt you!" The
arms loosened and Helen sprang free.

Helen did not like strangers, but she
was curious about them. So now she
came back. She patted her hand across
Annie Sullivan's face and down over her
dusty travelling dress.

Annie laughed. "I can see that she

doesn't like to be touched. But she isn't a bit frightened, is she?"

Mr. Keller took his time answering. "No, Miss Annie," he finally said. "And I think that you will sometimes find that that's a problem."

Early the next morning Mrs. Keller led Helen into Annie Sullivan's room. It was time for the first lesson to begin. Helen didn't know this of course. So she just wandered around the room — touching all the new things the stranger had brought with her.

One of the first things she found was Annie's suitcase, lying open on the bed. Her curious hands plunged inside. And what was this? Helen's face lit up. She knew right away. It was a doll! She had others in her room. She wanted this one too. Helen snatched it out of the suitcase and hugged it close.

"It's a present for Helen from the little blind girls at Perkins," Annie told Mrs. Keller. "And it's also as good a place to begin as any."

She picked up Helen's hand. Helen started to tug away. But then she stopped. What was the stranger doing with her hand?

"This is called the finger alphabet," Annie explained to Helen's mother. "It's a way of talking to the deaf. I am making the shapes of the letters D-O-L-L into Helen's palm. Then I will take her hand and run it over the real doll in her arms. You see, first the word — and then what the word stands for. The word — and what it stands for again. I am simply trying to connect these two things in her mind."

"Look, Miss Annie!" Mrs. Keller cried. "Helen is making those movements too!"

And she was. Slowly, Helen Keller's fingers were making the shapes of the word D-O-L-L.

"What a quick little monkey you are," Annie murmured — and she bent down to help. Then she saw the look on Mrs. Keller's face.

"No, no! You must not get your hopes up so soon," Annie said quickly. "Helen has learned how to make the shapes of her first word. And very fast too. But she does not know that these shapes stand for all the dolls in the world. She does not know they have *meaning*."

Now Annie turned back to Helen. "So come on! Let's go on with the lesson."

Annie pulled the doll out of Helen's arms. She meant to give it back as soon as Helen spelled the word D-O-L-L again. But Helen didn't know this. All she knew was that the stranger was taking her doll away from her. And she wanted it back!

Again and again Helen reached for the doll. But her hand only touched empty air. She began to growl.

"Look out, Miss Annie," Mrs. Keller cried. But her warning came too late. Helen came charging. Her fist shot out. And she hit Annie Sullivan right in the mouth.

Helen could not hear her pain-filled cry. But she could feel the stranger jerk away. She smiled.

"Oh, let her have the doll," Mrs. Keller

cried. "It's the only way to calm her."

"No," Annie said. "There is another way. Helen must learn self-control."

"But Helen doesn't know what self-control is," Mrs. Keller answered. "She doesn't know how to keep her temper."

"Then that is the first lesson I must teach her," Annie Sullivan said. "For I do not think I can teach her anything else until I do."

Helen came charging again. But this time Annie was ready for her. She grabbed Helen's arms and hung on as tight as she could.

Helen kicked and screamed for quite a while. Then suddenly she went limp. "So, my girl," Annie said. "Have you had enough? Are you ready to go on?"

But it was a trick. As soon as Annie let go, Helen ran from the room. She would not come back all day.

Helen slept as well as ever that night. But Annie Sullivan didn't. She lay in bed and thought about Helen. Annie had been in Tuscumbia for only one day. But already she knew that everyone in this house felt too sorry for Helen. They had let her have her own way for years. Now she was badly spoiled.

"And that must stop," Annie thought. "For how can I reach her mind while she rants and rages like a wild animal? No, I must be loving — but firm. That's the best way to help Helen."

The Worst Fight of All

HELEN didn't know that Annie had come to help her. All she knew was that a stranger was trying to make her do things she did not understand, things she did *not* want to do. So six-year-old Helen did what she had been doing for years. She fought back.

She ran. She hid. She fought with sly tricks. One day Helen locked Annie in her room and hid the key. Helen's mother tried to get Helen to show where she had hidden the key. Helen just turned away — and smiled. Finally her father had to put a ladder up to the window and carry Annie down like a sack of potatoes.

But most of the time Helen fought with her fists. Day by day those fights grew worse. Helen was strong. But the stranger was stronger. Helen could fight for hours. But this stranger never seemed to tire!

"It's that little bit of strength that's going to save us," Annie Sullivan wrote a friend one day, ". . . if she doesn't kill us both first!"

Annie tried to keep cheerful. It was not always easy. One day Helen's hand brushed against Annie's face — and came away wet. Helen didn't know what tears meant, so she just turned away.

Then came the worst fight of all.

Helen had the table manners of a pig. She knew how to use her knife and fork and spoon. But she liked to use her hands instead.

She began each meal in her own chair, but she never stayed there for long. Most of the time she wandered from place to place — grabbing what she wanted from other people's plates.

Annie watched with horror as Helen stuffed other people's food in her mouth. But Annie didn't say anything — so long as Helen stayed away from her.

Then one morning Helen stopped behind Annie's chair. Her nose wriggled to sort out the smells. What was that on the stranger's plate? She sniffed again. Then she knew. It was sausage! And Helen loved sausage.

But did she dare? Helen stood there

for a moment. Then she touched her way round the table again. At every chair she stopped and sniffed. Everyone else's sausage was gone. Now here she was, back at the stranger's plate.

Once more the delicious smell of sausage came drifting up to her. It was just too much. Out flashed Helen's hand. Down came the stranger's on top of it!

Helen tried to jerk free. The stranger held on tight. And one by one she peeled Helen's fingers away from the sausage.

"Oh, let her have it just this once," Mr. Keller said. "She doesn't know any better."

Annie shook her head. "She must learn that other people have rights too," she answered.

So the fight began. Helen kicked and screamed. She pounded her fists on the floor. Helen's mother and father hated to see her this upset. They got up and left the room quickly. Annie locked the door behind them. Then she went back to her chair.

For a while Annie sat. Helen rolled and raged on the floor. But Helen was growing hungrier every minute. What was the stranger doing? Was there any sausage left on her plate? Finally Helen got up to find out.

She sniffed — and yes! There was some sausage left. Helen's hand crept forward.

Annie pushed it back. Helen's hand crept forward again. Annie pushed it away again.

Helen lost her temper. But this time she didn't yell and scream. She just pinched the stranger's arm as hard as she could.

Annie slapped back — hard. Helen shook herself. That hurt! But it didn't stop her. Helen pinched the stranger again. And once more Annie slapped Helen. *Pinch – slap. Pinch – slap.* "I can keep this up as long as you can," Annie Sullivan said.

Suddenly Helen wheeled away. She touched her way around the table again. But all the chairs were empty! Everyone else was gone!

Helen raced for the door. She tugged on it as hard as she could. It would not open! Then Helen knew. She was locked in with the stranger. And all the under-standing arms were gone!

Helen backed against the wall. She wanted to stay as far away from Annie as she could. But she was growing more and more hungry. Finally Helen edged her way back to the table again and began to eat — with her fingers.

Annie sighed — and put a spoon in Helen's hand. Helen held it for a moment. Then she threw it as hard as she could across the room.

Annie pulled Helen out of her chair and dragged her across the room to pick up the spoon. Then she plunked her back in her seat again.

"Now you're going to eat that oat-meal," Annie said. "And with that spoon!"

Helen kicked. She screamed. She wrig-gled like an eel. But inch by inch Annie Sullivan forced the spoon up to Helen's

mouth. She forced Helen to swallow one spoonful. And then another. Then Annie began to relax.

Too soon! Helen jerked free. She threw the spoon at Annie. Annie ducked. And everything started all over again.

But this time Helen didn't fight so hard. She was so hungry, and so tired. This time, when Annie let go, Helen kept right on eating until finally her bowl was empty, her breakfast all gone.

But so was the morning. The sun was

high overhead when Annie finally unlocked the door. Smells of lunch filled the house.

Annie led Helen outside to wander in the garden. She went to her room to think. Things could not go on this way much longer. Something would have to be done — and fast.

But what? Annie paced back and forth across her room. Slowly a plan began to form in her mind. But first she would have to talk to Helen's mother. It was not going to be easy to find the right words.

W-A-T-E-R!

"Miss Kate, I want to take Helen away with me," Annie said.

"What?" gasped Mrs. Keller.

"I must teach Helen to mind me," Annie explained. "But I can't do it here in this house. Every time I try, she turns to you and away from me. More and more she will think of me as an enemy. Then everything will be lost."

Mrs. Keller didn't say *no*. But she didn't say *yes* either.

Annie tried again. "It will just be for a while. Just until Helen learns that I am a part of her life too."

"There is a little garden house near here," Mrs. Keller said slowly. But she still didn't say *yes*.

Annie leaned forward. "I know it is a gamble," she said softly. "It is also our last chance."

Last chance. Mrs. Keller sat very still for a moment. Then she nodded *yes*.

So Helen and Annie went to live in the little house on the other side of the garden. At first Helen kicked and screamed and fought as hard as ever. But slowly there came a change.

Helen still fought, but not as hard. And not as often. Sometimes she would even let the stranger hold her for a moment. Then one day Helen did not fight at all.

"The first great step has been taken," Annie wrote a friend. "Helen has learned how to mind!"

But Helen still didn't know what words were. Day after day Annie spelled into Helen's hand. And Helen learned to make more and more shapes back. By the end of March — in less than two weeks — she could make twenty-one word-shapes. The next day she learned how to make eight more. But she didn't know what they meant. It was just a game she played with her hands.

April 5, 1887, began like any other day. After breakfast Annie began to spell into Helen's hand. But Helen was restless this morning. The window was open and the smells of spring came pouring in. Besides, Helen was growing very tired of this game with no meaning!

She tugged on Annie's skirt, then

pointed to the window. Her meaning was very clear. *Let's go out!*

At first Annie tried to go on with the lesson. But Helen's face darkened. Her hands clenched into fists. She was holding her new doll in her lap. Now she picked it up and threw it as hard as she could. It broke into many small pieces.

Helen didn't care. She didn't love the doll anyway. She felt the stranger sweep up the pieces. Then the stranger handed her her hat. So Helen knew they were going outside after all. She skipped and danced by the stranger's side. No more lessons! She was getting her own way!

Or was she?

Helen and Annie wandered in the garden for a while. Then they came to an old pump house. Helen liked to play in its cool dampness. She ran inside.

In the middle of the floor stood a

pump. Annie Sullivan began to move its handle up and down. Soon a steady stream of water came pouring out of its spout. Now she took Helen's hand and held it under the cool flow. W-A-T-E-R, she spelled into Helen's wet palm.

At first Helen pulled away. But then suddenly she stopped. A new light seemed to come to her face.

Annie saw the look. W-A-T-E-R, she spelled quickly. W-A-T-E-R!

W-A-T-. . . Helen began to spell back.

And with each movement her face grew brighter. For suddenly she knew! The shapes that the stranger was making with her fingers *did* have a meaning! *Everything had a name.* Everything in the whole world had a name! And she could learn them all!

"Oh, yes, Helen," Annie whispered. "That's *it!*" And she bent down to hug the shaking little girl.

But Helen pulled away. She didn't have time for *that* now! She dropped to the ground and thumped on it hard. *Name it!* she was demanding. So — laughing, sobbing — Annie did.

Helen paused for a moment. She fluttered off the word on her fingers. She nodded. Then she whirled away again. In the next few minutes she learned six new words. And she knew what they meant!

Then suddenly Helen stopped. She thumped herself across the head. Annie burst out laughing. "Yes, dear," she said. "There's a word for you too." And she bent down and spelled H-E-L-E-N into the little girl's hand.

Helen had a name at last!

Now Helen reached out and patted Annie's arm. At first Annie thought she was just saying "thank you." But Helen wanted something more than that. She patted Annie's arm again.

"Oh," said Annie. "So you want to know that too." And Annie spelled T-E-A-C-H-E-R into Helen's waiting hand.

A few minutes later two new people came out of the pump house. The wild little girl was gone. And so was the stranger. Now Helen Keller and Teacher walked hand in hand.

So Much to Learn

HELEN wanted to know the names for everything she touched. And Teacher gave them to her. Before the first day was over Helen learned how to make thirty word shapes. Before the first month was over she knew how to spell one hundred words.

From early morning until late at night Helen spelled the words she knew. She spelled until her eyelids drooped and her fingers could hardly make the shapes.

"You really should slow her down," a worried friend said, "or she will hurt her brain." Teacher just smiled. She knew that nothing could stop Helen now.

By the middle of June Helen knew more than four hundred words. But there was one important word she did not know. Helen was seven years old now. But for more than five of those years she had been blind and deaf. During those five years she had forgotten how to *laugh.*

One day Teacher came bursting into Helen's room. She was laughing as hard as she could. She grabbed Helen's hand and held it to her upturned lips. L-A-U-G-H, she spelled into Helen's hand.

Teacher picked Helen up and swung her around. They hopped, they skipped, they jumped around the room. Helen didn't know it — but Teacher was leading her through the motions of happiness. And all the while she spelled L-A-U-G-H.

Now Teacher began to tickle Helen. Suddenly Helen smiled. Her smile grew wider. A chuckle escaped. Finally — with a great whoop — she began to laugh.

Helen's mother and father had heard the noise coming from her room. They had come to the door to watch. Mrs. Keller leaned her head against her husband's shoulder. "Oh, Arthur," she whispered. *"Helen's laughing.* I never thought I'd hear that sound again."

Soon Helen was ready to take her next big step forward. It was time, Teacher said, for her to learn how to read.

Teacher got out a big card. On the card were printed the twenty-six letters of the alphabet. Each letter stood up from the background so that you could

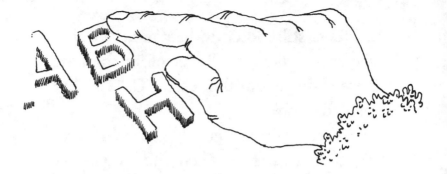

feel it. This was how the blind had to learn how to read — with their hands.

Teacher took one of Helen's hands and put it on the raised letter **A**. At the same time she made the sign for the letter **A** into Helen's other hand. At first Helen frowned and looked puzzled. She understood what was happening in one hand — but what was happening under her other?

Teacher didn't try to explain. She just moved Helen's finger on to the next letter on the card. **B**, she spelled at the same time into Helen's other hand.

Helen still didn't understand. But now she moved her own finger on to the next raised shape on the card. C, Teacher spelled quickly.

Helen kept on going. Teacher kept right up with her. Then suddenly — between one letter and another — Helen stopped. She began to smile. For suddenly she understood.

Before the day was over Helen learned all the letters of the alphabet. She was ready to move on to words. That night a tired but happy Annie Sullivan sat down and wrote a letter. "Something tells me," she wrote, "that I am going to succeed beyond my wildest dreams."

Helen and Teacher did not spend all their time hunched over alphabet sheets and word cards.

A long-eared rabbit wriggling his nose

. . . a smooth-shelled bug crawling across her palm . . . the smell of wild grapes — and the sweet-tart taste of them too. There were so many other lessons to be learned outside — lessons from life.

Helen planted a seed in the newly plowed earth. A few days later she felt a plant coming up in its place. She learned the names of the trees that grew on her father's land — and how to tell them apart by touch.

One hot day Helen and Teacher were coming home from a walk. They stopped under a tree to rest. "Would you like to climb the tree?" Teacher asked. Helen nodded *yes*. So Teacher helped her up.

Then Teacher had another idea. "It's so cool here," she spelled, "why don't we eat lunch up in the tree? I'll go back to the house and make some sandwiches. You wait for me here."

Helen nodded happily. She thought it was fun to wait up in the tree. But suddenly a change came over the day. The air grew cooler. All the heat seemed to be fading away. Helen frowned. The sun must be hiding behind a cloud, she thought.

And what was that strange smell coming up from the ground? Helen took a deep sniff. Then she knew. It was the smell that always came right before a really big storm.

The wind began to blow. Helen felt a thudding all around. This was thunder. But to Helen it seemed as if a giant were dropping something heavy nearby. And he was coming closer all the time!

Teacher! Teacher! Teacher! Helen's fingers fluttered frantically. But the wind only blew harder. And nobody came.

A branch broke over Helen's head.

Twigs splattered down around her. "Jump!" Helen thought. But what if she did? Would she go flying off into space? Would she crash to the ground?

Helen decided to hang on. But her fingers were slipping! She could not hold on much longer! Then Helen felt the most wonderful thing in the world — Teacher's arms lifting her down from the tree.

One day Teacher put an egg into Helen's hand. "Hold it carefully," she spelled. Helen was puzzled. She already knew what eggs were. She had two every morning for breakfast. What was so different about this one?

"Wait and see," Teacher spelled.

The first thing Helen noticed was that the egg was very warm. Then it began to do very strange things — it began to

quiver, to shake in her hand! Now she could feel something *chip, chipping* against the inside of the egg shell. Something was *alive* in there. And it was trying to get out!

Helen's mouth opened into a silent O of wonder as the egg shell began to crack. A few minutes later a baby chick was born in her hand.

But what about things Helen could not hold in her hand? What about things that were too big? Or far away? Or that happened long ago? How could she learn about them? Helen had to trust other people to tell her about the colors she would never see and the sounds she would never hear.

And what about ideas — thoughts — with no shapes at all? Helen remembered all her life the first time she understood an idea.

One day Teacher asked her a very hard question. Helen tried to think of the answer. She tried as hard as she could.

Teacher leaned forward. She tapped Helen's forehead. T-H-I-N-K! she spelled at the same time. And suddenly Helen knew. That's what was happening inside her head. She was *thinking!*

Helen learned so many hard things that first summer. But she didn't know they were hard. To seven-year-old Helen Keller it was simply a magic time, a time when the world came to life in her hand.

A Time to Move On

As soon as Helen woke up she knew, *Something wonderful is going to happen today.* It was a fine, crisp fall day. But Helen knew it wasn't that. Then she remembered. The circus had come to Tuscumbia. And Teacher was taking her today!

Helen's nose began to twitch even before they got to the circus grounds. Hot sausages, meat pies, onions, lemonade, coffee, spun sugar candy — what wonderful smells were coming from there! Helen tugged on Teacher's hand. *Hurry!* she meant.

The circus people soon heard about the little deaf and blind girl who had come to their show. They wanted to see that she had a good time. And they thought of a way. They made Helen a part of the show!

She sat in the lap of a lady called "The Oriental Princess," and rode around the ring in a flower-covered cart. She touched the spangled dresses of the pretty dancing girls. She ran her hands over the funny-faced clowns.

But best of all were the animals. After the show was over the circus people led Helen to where the animals lived in their cages.

"Is she afraid of animals?" one of the circus people asked.

"No," Teacher answered. "Helen likes to touch anything that moves." And the animals seemed to sense that Helen Keller was different from other boys and girls. So they were especially gentle with her.

Helen patted a lion. She shook hands with a bear. She fed peanuts to an elephant and asked, "Why does he have such a long nose?" A leopard licked her hand with his rough tongue.

A man held Helen up to feel the ears of a giraffe. A snake curled itself around her arm. She played with the monkeys. And the monkeys played with her!

One monkey stole her hair ribbon. Another tried to snatch the flowers out of her hat. Helen laughed so hard she almost began to choke. "I don't know who had the better time," the animal keeper said later, "Helen, or my monkeys."

Then it was December. "Do you know what happens this month?" Teacher spelled. Helen shook her head.

"Christmas!"

But Helen's face stayed blank. She was seven years old, but up until now Christmas had never had any meaning for her. So everything was new.

Teacher spelled out Christmas stories for Helen and the words of old songs. She taught Helen to play Christmas games. Helen helped her mother bake huge batches of Christmas cookies and candies and cakes. She made presents for everyone in the house.

Finally Christmas Eve came. Helen was so excited she could not go to sleep. "You'll have to," Teacher spelled. "Or Santa Claus won't come."

So Helen closed her eyes — and smiled. "Santa Claus will think girl is asleep," she spelled.

But finally Helen did go to sleep. And the next thing she knew the day was there! "Merry Christmas!" she spelled into Teacher's hand. "Wake up!"

Teacher yawned and rubbed her eyes. "Helen Keller," she scolded, "do you know what time it is? It isn't even light out yet!" But of course that didn't matter to Helen. The dark was her familiar world.

What a Christmas Day that was! Helen found surprises everywhere — on the table, on the chairs, under the Christmas tree downstairs. "I could hardly walk," she wrote later, "without stumbling over a bit of Christmas wrapped up in tissue paper." When Teacher handed her a live canary in a cage, Helen thought she would burst with Christmas joy.

Mrs. Keller watched her daughter playing happily. There were tears in her eyes as she turned toward Teacher.

"Miss Annie," Helen's mother said, "I have thanked God every day for sending you to us. But I did not know until this morning what a blessing you have been."

One spring day of 1888 Teacher received an important letter. It was from Mr. Michael Anagnos, the director of Perkins Institute. Annie Sullivan had studied there as a child. And that was where she had learned how to help Helen. Now Mr. Anagnos invited them both to come visit his school.

Teacher frowned as she read the letter. This was probably a good idea. Helen was asking harder and harder questions every day. Some Teacher could not answer. Soon Helen would need more teachers.

But was Helen ready to go into the world? After all, only a year had gone by since Helen had learned there was a real world at all. Would people think she was still too different? Would they pity her too much?

Teacher thought back over all Helen had learned how to do. She could talk with her fingers, and listen with the palm of her hand. She knew just as many words as any other eight-year-old child. She could read raised-print books. She could write with a pencil. She was even learning how to read and write in braille — the raised-dot language of the blind.

And there were some things Helen could do *better* than other people. She could tell the difference between a dog's bark of welcome and his first warning growl — by putting her hand on his throat. She knew when she was in a room with books in it — by the smell of paper and ink. She could tell people apart by touch. Helen said some people had "frosty finger tips" and she did not like to touch them. Others, she said, "have hands that warm my heart."

Yes, Teacher finally decided, their first year of discovery was over. It was time to move on.

"I Am Not Dumb Now!"

Teacher decided to take Helen North for the summer. Helen remembered that trip for the rest of her life. First she and Teacher went to Perkins Institute in Boston, Massachusetts. They stayed there for a month.

The teachers at Perkins all made a fuss over Helen — she wasn't sure why, but she liked it all the same. She played happily with the boys and girls at the Institute for hours each day. But best of all were the books.

Perkins Institute was a school for the blind. So all of its books were in braille or raised print. Oh, the joy of it! Row after row of books — and every one she could read for herself!

Helen already knew how important books were going to be in her life. "They tell me so much that is interesting about things I cannot see," she said. "And they are never tired or troubled like people."

But Helen didn't spend all her time reading books. There were so many other interesting things to do. Teacher took her to a play. Helen couldn't see or hear what was going on, of course. But Teacher spelled everything into her hand.

Helen rode on her first steamboat. The little ship was full of life and motion. The

rumble of machinery under her feet made Helen think of thunder.

One day Teacher took Helen to the nearby town of Plymouth and Helen stood on Plymouth Rock — where almost three hundred years before, she was told, the first Pilgrims had landed in America.

After Perkins Institute closed for the summer, Teacher took Helen to visit a friend who lived by the sea. Helen played happily in the warm, soft sand. She loved to sit on a rock and feel wave after wave wash over her legs. Soon she was toasty brown.

Then the weather turned cool. It was fall and time to go home again. Helen could hardly wait to be with her mother and father again. She had so many things to tell them about this first trip into the world. "It was a time when I lived myself into all things," Helen later wrote.

One day, soon after Helen and Teacher had returned to Tuscumbia, Teacher spelled, "Come and sit beside me. I have a new book to read you. It's called *Little Lord Fauntleroy* and I think you will like it very much."

So Helen snuggled down beside Teacher. She held out her hand — and Teacher began to read. Oh, what an exciting story! At first Teacher tried to stop and explain the hard words. But Helen only wanted her to *go on, go on!*

Teacher spelled for a long time. But then she began to slow down. Finally she stopped. "Just a little bit more," Helen begged. But Teacher shook her head.

"My fingers are tired," she spelled. "I have to rest them a while." And she put back her head and closed her eyes.

Helen nodded. She knew that Teacher did not really mean that her fingers were tired. She knew that Teacher really meant her eyes were tired. For once Teacher had been blind too — almost as blind as Helen.

Teacher had had operations on her eyes, and now she could see a little. But her eyes were still very weak. Often she got terrible headaches. And most of the time she had to wear dark glasses to keep out the bright light of the sun.

So Helen tried to be patient. She sat as still as she could and waited for what seemed a very long time. But oh! she wanted to know what happened next in the story. So finally her hand crept out. "Teacher?" she spelled softly.

Teacher's hand curled around hers. But it did not answer back. Helen sighed. Teacher was fast asleep. Suddenly Helen felt terribly, terribly alone.

She reached out and brushed her hand

across the book — still open in Teacher's lap. There were words on those pages. But not for her! Never for her! Oh, why did she have to be so different?

And then — in that moment of bitterness — the beginning of an idea came to Helen's mind. She knew she would never be able to see. She would never be able to hear. But there was one thing she might be able to do like other people. As the days went by Helen began to ask questions.

"How do blind girls know what to say with their mouths?"

"Do deaf children ever learn how to speak?"

Finally Helen's idea came bursting out. "Teacher, I want to talk like other people! Teach me to talk with my mouth!"

At first Teacher said *no*. She thought that this was an impossible dream. "Blind children can hear," she spelled gently. "Deaf boys and girls can see other people's lips move."

But Helen was growing more and more unhappy talking with her hands. Most people could not understand this way of talking. Besides, Helen's mind had grown so much, her thoughts came so fast one after another, that her fingers could not keep up.

Helen was nine years old now. Often she spelled so fast, people had to tell her, "Slow down. Your fingers are all tangled. You'll have to say it again." And still thoughts piled up in her brain.

So Helen would not take *no* for an answer. She was sure they would find a way — somehow! Finally Teacher gave in. "But I am not trained to teach you myself," she spelled. "We will have to find someone else who can."

Finally Teacher took Helen back to Boston, Massachusetts. There, at the Horace Mann School, Miss Sarah Fuller began to teach Helen how to speak with her mouth.

Helen put her hand on Miss Fuller's face. She touched her lips and tongue. She felt the way Miss Fuller's throat vibrated when she made the simple sound *ah*.

Then it was Helen's turn. Her hands flew to her own face. She tried to put her lips and tongue in the same position. She tried to make her throat vibrate into the same sound *ah*.

"Good, Helen," Miss Fuller spelled. Oh, Helen was proud: She had taken her first step forward.

But it was only a baby step. Again and again Helen learned how to make a sound — only to forget it. Then she had to start all over again.

Practice, practice, practice! Helen practiced until her mouth and throat were swollen and sore. And still so many sounds slipped away. "Oh, this is too hard! I can not do the impossible!" she would cry to herself then.

But she refused to give up. And little by little she got better. Until one day Helen opened her mouth and said in a growly voice, *"I a-amm n-o-oottttttT d-d-duuummm-bB n-nooow."*

I am not dumb now. Five broken words. Two were spoken in a whisper. Three were spoken in a shout. She would have to practice all her life. She would never learn how to speak very clearly. But a miracle had happened all the same. Helen Keller had learned how to talk with her mouth.

College

MORE and more people were hearing about Helen. Newspaper reporters wrote stories about her. A shipbuilder in Maine named a ship after her. Important people everywhere were becoming her friends. Twelve-year-old Helen was even invited to the White House to meet the President of the United States.

Most of the time Helen was not visiting such important people. Most of the time she was doing much simpler things — things she liked just as well.

When she was home in Tuscumbia she rode her horse, Black Beauty. She took her dogs for walks in the sweet-smelling woods. And she spent hours every day close to her mother's side.

A friend gave Helen a bicycle called a tandem — a bicycle built for two. Helen sat behind and pushed the pedals. Someone else sat up front and steered.

One summer Helen learned how to swim. She even worked out a way to swim by herself. She tied one end of a rope around her waist. She tied the other end of the rope around a rock or a tree. Then she could swim safely, and when she was tired she followed the rope to shore.

Helen learned how to row a boat by herself too. She could tell where she was by the different smells of grasses and bushes that grew on the bank.

Helen and Teacher usually spent the summer months at home in Tuscumbia. They spent most of the winter months studying in Boston or visiting friends in the countryside nearby.

How Helen loved to be outside on those cold wintry days. She loved to feel the air stinging her face. She liked to zip down the snowy hills on the back of a sled. Helen helped her friends build snowmen. She felt snowflakes melt in her hand as Teacher described their many different shapes.

In the evenings Helen and Teacher roasted apples or popped popcorn or played quiet games in front of the fire. Sometimes they played cards. Helen had to have special cards of course. Each card had a different pattern of raised bumps on it so she could tell them apart. Other times they played checkers. The black checkers were flat on top. The red checkers were round.

Best of all were the evenings when friends came to call. Teacher spelled what they were saying to Helen. But every once in a while Teacher grew so interested herself that she forgot to spell. Then Helen would say loudly, "What's going on?" Helen Keller hated to be left out of anything.

But Helen had less and less time for romps in the snow or quiet evenings by the fire. Now she had a new goal. "I want to go to college when I grow up," twelve-year-old Helen announced one day. "And the college I want to go to is Harvard."

Teacher felt like saying *no*. In college Helen would have to keep up with students who could see their books and hear their teachers talk. Helen was very, very bright. Yet how could anyone — no matter how bright — possibly do that?

But Teacher also thought that Helen had the right to try. So all she said was, "Not Harvard, Helen. That s a boys' school." And they started to work.

Latin, Greek, German, French, geography, zoology, history, biology, mathematics. There were so many things to learn before Helen could even try to get into college.

Sometimes she studied with other teachers. Sometimes she and Teacher stayed at home and studied by themselves. Wherever she was she worked many long hours every day. Six busy years passed. At last Helen was ready.

Then she discovered a very upsetting fact. Helen Keller was ready for college. But college wasn't ready for her!

Helen wanted to go to Radcliffe, a very well known women's college. But the president of Radcliffe didn't want to take Helen. He thought she would cause too many problems. "You have come a long way," he told her, "but surely you will not be able to keep up with our girls."

Helen hated to be treated like this! She sat down and wrote a letter. "You must let me *try*," she wrote to the president of Radcliffe, "for a true soldier does not admit defeat before the battle."

Helen's spirit must have impressed the president of Radcliffe. He changed his mind. In the fall of 1900 Helen Keller entered Radcliffe College.

She had worked hard before. She

worked twice as hard now. Teacher always sat beside Helen in class and spelled into her hand what the teacher was saying. But sometimes her fingers could not keep up with his voice. Then Helen simply missed a part of the lesson.

Helen didn't have time to take notes. She had to remember everything without them.

When she took a test she could not look back over what she had written. She had to get everything right the very first time.

And there were so many books to read. Helen read braille and raised-print books until her finger tips bled. But most of the books were not in raised print. Teacher had to read these other books to her.

Poor Teacher. Her sick eyes grew red and sore. She never had time to rest them anymore. She almost lost her sight. But Teacher was stubborn too. She just held the books closer and read on.

And together they won! In the fall of 1904 Helen Keller stood in line with ninety-six other girls. She felt a rolled up piece of paper being put in her hand.

This was her diploma. Helen Keller had graduated *cum laude* — with honor — from Radcliffe College. She was the best educated deaf-blind person in the world.

The Busy Years

HELEN was very lucky. And she knew it. "My life is so rich in two things," she said, "friends and books."

But what about the other deaf and blind people who were not so lucky? Helen knew that many led lonely lives with no families and few friends. Often they were too poor to go to school.

Too often the blind never learned how to read with their hands. Too often the deaf were not taught to speak with their mouths. Their days were long and dull. "And life is made up of days," Helen Keller said.

Helen was twenty-four years old now. She had many more years to live. And she was determined to do something useful with those years. She decided to become a writer — she would write about the problems of the blind and the deaf.

But soon Helen found that most people wanted her to write only about herself. They were not interested in how to save a baby's eyes from blindness, or in a new kind of school for the deaf.

Helen kept on writing. But now she thought up another way to help. She decided to give lectures. She and Teacher would travel from town to town all across the country giving speeches about the problems of the blind and the deaf.

First Teacher came on stage and spoke about their early years together. Then Helen — in her blurred voice — told the audience what it was like to be deaf and blind.

About the deaf, Helen Keller said, "They are surrounded by silence — never to be broken by a word or a song or the sigh of a breeze."

About the blind — who Helen felt were the loneliest people in the world — she said, "They stare into the dark. And nothing but the dark stares back."

Helen also gave advice. "I who am blind can only give one hint to you who can see. Use your eyes as if tomorrow you would go blind. Do the same with all your other senses. Hear the song of a bird as if tomorrow you would go deaf. Touch everything as if tomorrow you would never be able to touch anything again. Smell the flowers, taste every bit of food as if tomorrow you would never smell or taste again."

Finally Helen answered questions from the audience. Some of the questions people asked were serious ones. Others were just plain silly.

"Can you tell the difference between colors?" she was asked again and again.

"Sometimes I feel blue and sometimes I see red," Helen would always answer.

"Do you sleep with your eyes open?"

"I never stayed awake to see!"

The busy years were passing. And Helen Keller's teacher was growing old. One day she said to Helen, "I'm sorry, dear, but I can't make any more trips with you."

Then Teacher fell sick and had to spend most of her time in bed. "You must get well," a friend begged. "Helen would be nothing without you."

Teacher frowned. "Then I would have failed," she answered. She had worked all her life to make Helen Keller free — free even of her.

Annie Sullivan died on October 19, 1936. Helen had faced other pain in her life, but nothing like this. Her thoughts flew back over fifty years to the day when a young Annie had come to turn a wild animal-child into a little girl.

"That was the most important day of my life," Helen said many times. "It was my soul's birthday — the day my teacher came to me." And now she was gone!

"A big piece of my heart has just died too," Helen said. How could she go on living without Teacher by her side?

But there was still so much to do. With the help of a wonderful woman named Polly Thomson, Helen continued to give her lectures. She went all over the United States. More and more often she went to foreign lands too.

Then in 1939 a terrible war broke out in Europe. It spread to many countries of the world. Soon the men of the United States, too, were fighting in the Second World War.

Many were wounded in the battles. Some were blinded and deafened. Others were crippled, or lost arms and legs. Often these men did not want to go on living. President Franklin Roosevelt asked Helen Keller to visit them. He wanted her to help them see that life was still worth living.

In the next few years Helen went from hospital to hospital, all across the land. And everywhere the men welcomed her.

"Gee," one soldier said, "I read about you in school. I never thought I'd be blind myself."

Helen didn't try to fool these men with words of easy cheer. "Of course you will have bitter moments," she said. "I do too. Of course there will be days when you will feel restless and lonely and cheated. All I can tell you is, live as much like other people as you can. Keep your life full of books and work and friends. I do — and look how well it has worked for me."

When Helen wasn't busy working, she filled her days with fun. She was always ready to go to new places and try new things. "Life is an adventure," Helen Keller said, "or it is nothing."

She rode in the cab of a train. She visited a coal mine deep in the earth. The Stony Tribe of Indians made her a

blood-sister. She flew in an open aircraft. She loved that. "We're riding on the wind!" she cried.

Helen went on the roughest camping trips. She visited the great cities of the world. She could tell many of these cities apart by their smells. The Italian section of New York smelled of garlic and salami and cheese. Paris smelled of perfume and powder, wine and tobacco. St. Louis smelled of beer.

Finally Helen Keller grew old and frail. She did not travel anymore. She went home to her house in Westport, Connecticut. Her days were quiet now. But she still kept very busy.

Helen got up before five every morning. First she made a simple breakfast for herself. Then she went for a walk. Helen would find her way by holding onto wires that stretched all around her land.

"I cannot see or hear but I find hundreds of things to interest me," she said. She loved to feel the smooth skin of a silver birch tree or the rough shaggy bark of a pine. "If I'm lucky," she said, "I can put my hand on a small tree and feel it quiver as a bird sings in its branches."

Helen still worked six or seven hours a day at her desk. In the evenings friends often came to call. Late at night Helen usually read herself to sleep. Many times someone would go past her dark room and hear her fingers brushing over raised letters or rows of braille dots.

She lived until she was eighty-seven years old. Then on June 1, 1968, Helen Keller slipped away into the dark silence.

Helen Keller was dead. But her spirit lives on. As she said so many times, "The best and most beautiful things in the world can not be seen or even touched. They must be felt with the heart."

Helen Keller
1880 – 1968

Helen Keller and her teacher, Annie Sullivan

Helen Keller reading with her fingers

Helen Keller wanted to do all the things that other people could do—and more. She was a good horseback rider.

SCHOLASTIC BIOGRAPHY